The Champion Spirit

"Healing from Sexual, Mental, and Physical Abuse with Strength and Purpose"

Disclaimer Notice

By reading this document, you acknowledge and agree to the following terms:

Before You Go Any Further — Please Read This. What you're holding isn't just a book—it's my truth. I lived through years of silence, abuse, and pain—the kind most people never speak about out loud. I hope my experiences give you hope for freedom.

I'm not a therapist, a doctor, or a lawyer. I don't have a degree hanging on the wall. I have real-life experience—what it feels like to wake up hurting and keep going. I wrote this not because I had all the answers but because I found something that worked, and I believe someone out there might need to hear it.

This book contains honest and heartfelt writing that draws on my own experiences. It's not clinical advice or a professional treatment plan, but it's what helped me heal.

If you choose to read on, you're doing so by your own choice, and you understand the following:

This is for Insight, Not Instruction. I wrote this book to inspire, share my growth, and offer support. It is not meant to replace therapy, counseling, or professional help. Please seek a licensed expert if you're in crisis or need guidance. Remember, you're not alone in this journey.

Not Professional Advice. Nothing in this book should be considered medical, psychological, legal, or financial advice. This is my story—not a substitute for professional services or consultation.

Father

I come to your throne with a humble heart and kneel before you, **God**. I do this not in my own strength, but in your grace and mercy. I am nothing without You. All healing, restoration, and power flow from Your hands alone, **God**. **Lord**, I lift up every soul before You now. You see their wounds, both spoken and unspoken. You know the battles they fight in silence. You know the pain that still echoes in their hearts. I ask You, in Your perfect love, to touch them gently and completely. Heal what is broken.

Restore what has been stolen, Lord, for You see every loss.

And renew what has grown weary, that **Your** strength may fill what is depleted.

Let **Your** peace settle in their minds, bringing calm amidst their storms.

May **Your** strength rise in their bodies, giving them endurance each day.

Let **Your** truth wash over their hearts, lifting burdens with clarity. Where there is fear, Lord, replace it with courage and unwavering faith. Where there is shame, let dignity and **Your** acceptance take root. Where there is sorrow, replace it with hope. Where there is confusion, replace it with clarity. **Father**, remind them that they are seen, valued, and deeply loved by **You**. Let them feel **Your** presence in a way that brings comfort and confidence. Let **Your** Spirit move through every part of their life—mind, body, and soul. I ask that You surround them with **Your** protection, guide their steps, and give them rest where they are tired. May **Your** healing flow not only into them but also through them, so they become a light to others who are still hurting.

Lord, I do not claim this prayer by my authority, but only by **Yours**. You are a healer. You are a restorer.

You are the giver of life. And with gratitude and trust, I place every heart into **Your** loving hands.

In **Jesus'** name,

Amen.

Table of Contents

I know what's happening in your mind right now.

The doubt is creeping in, isn't it? You're staring at these four steps, and that voice inside is whispering: "This isn't for me. I'm too broken. Too far gone."

Trust me, I understand. And there's something you need to hear.

The truth I learned in those shadows, the truth I carry like a torch is that you are not too broken to heal. I've walked through that same valley of doubt, felt that same crushing weight of hopelessness, and I'm here to tell you with every fiber of my being - this works. It works because it must. It works because you deserve it to. It works because your story, like mine, refuses to end in shadows.

So, here's my promise, my vow to you. Yes, you.

Give these four steps just ten minutes a day for 90 days. Your mind will fight back with everything it has, throwing up walls of resistance and doubt. When it does, return to this book.

These steps work. They work no matter how broken you feel. Each one has been battle-tested in the trenches of trauma. They worked for someone who was told they shouldn't even be alive, and they'll work for you too. It doesn't matter how shattered you feel. It doesn't matter how many pieces you think you're in. The champion spirit lives within you, waiting.

I know what it feels like to be the only one who truly understands the depths of your own pain, to carry the burden of childhood trauma silently, fearing that if you dare voice your feelings, you'll be seen as less of a man.

From age 5 to age 12, I was sexually abused by two different men. The shame I carried made me feel weak. I was terrified other men would judge me and see me as gay or broken. I lived with the constant fear others could somehow sense the agony and self-loathing I harbored inside. I thought they would mock me and confirm all my worst fears. Every day I felt unworthy of happiness, trapped in a prison of shame. I know the raw, desperate feeling of barely hanging onto life, standing at the edge where suicide seems like the only escape from pain, a struggle that haunted me from my teenage years deep into adulthood. I understand that moment when darkness feels so consuming that ending everything seems like the only possible relief, when the weight of trauma presses so hard you can barely breathe.

But then, **God** revealed a path to healing. He showed me that I am more than the sum of my wounds. I am a man's man. I bear hunt, own a 4-wheel drive, and hold a Fifth Dan in Kenpo Karate. Even in my 50s, I still bench press over 400 pounds. I am strong, resilient, and worthy.

I was born and raised in the darkness. My self-will is one of accomplishment, rising above the darkness of trauma. My past will not define me; my unstoppable determination to heal, grow, and live the life I deserve. A man shaped by pain, not owned by it. A quiet warrior with nothing to prove and everything to live for.

This book isn't meant to be a deep dive into my life. Instead, it's a guide to healing, where elements of my journey serve as touchstones for your own path to recovery. These steps will transform your life and lead you to freedom from past trauma. I'm already walking that road, and I'm here to show you the way forward. The champion spirit lives within!

Raised in the depths of poverty by alcoholic parents, I was subjected to years of psychological and sexual abuse without ever hearing a single word of kindness. Trust was a foreign concept and love from my parents was never spoken, never felt. I never once heard the phrase, "I love you." It was as unfamiliar as a song never sung, its melody a distant hum from a world I had never known.

The first time I ever did hear those words, I was fifteen years old. I was at my best friend's house, and as we were leaving, his mother casually said, "I love you" to him. It struck me. It seemed fake, and from a very strange world of warmth and connection. I didn't know whether to envy my friend or pity him. Was this real, this word love? Or was I the strange one, standing there shocked by three simple words that seemed to carry the weight of an entire childhood I'd never heard or felt?

My childhood shattered at age **five** when my parents divorced. That's when the nightmare began, sexual abuse during weekend visits at my father's house by my older brother. When I wasn't there, a different horror awaited at my grandmother's, an older cousin. My mother worked night shifts, unaware that her child was being violated by two different men. This went on until I was twelve. I thought it was normal. I thought this was just what life was supposed to be.

The same year the abuse began, silence swallowed me whole; I couldn't hear. My **first-grade** teacher branded me "dumb." She thought I was not paying attention. She would use a ruler on my hand, speaking as she became frustrated when I couldn't understand. Four years passed before tubes in my ears gave me back sound, but by then crucial years of learning had slipped away forever. Those lost years still echo through my life today, a void I can never fill.

At seven, my mother married another alcoholic. The sexual abuse at my father's house was replaced by brutal beatings at my mother's. I became less than human in my own home, forced to sit on the couch, watching my stepfather eat, waiting like a stray dog for scraps. Only after he left could I enter the kitchen, my mother whispered, "Now you can eat."

My oldest brother was my only light, until he **was murdered** twelve days before my **fifteenth birthday**. That same summer I was arrested with three other boys for a robbery I did not commit. I slept through the robbery in the backseat of a stolen car. A month in the Youth Detention Center, a year of probation, and 80 hours of community service became my punishment for being in the wrong place at the wrong time.

Living with my father offered no escape. Drunk and cruel, he predicted daily that I'd be dead or in **prison by twenty-one.** My stepmother counted the days until she could throw me out and just three months shy of graduation, she did just that. **At seventeen**, I became homeless. No prom, no class ring, no celebration, just another kid from poverty wearing second-hand clothes and second-hand dreams.

Youth is supposed to fade gently into adulthood, but trauma doesn't read that script. **At seventeen**, I was playing grown-up, moving in with my girlfriend and working overtime to prove I could make it. Inside, though, I was still very much a wounded kid.

We married young and had our daughter. Then I found the workforce, where sweat and determination spoke louder than words. Here, 'normal' wasn't about fitting in; it was about showing up, pushing harder and reaching higher. Work wasn't just a job; it became my arena where each task was a chance to prove my worth to others and myself. I found peace in the rhythm of hard work and the satisfaction of a job well done. I earned respect through consistent effort and discovered that excellence doesn't ask for permission or validation. It simply demands dedication, and dedication I had in spades. Every morning became a new opportunity, and every challenge a chance to excel. I wasn't just working; I was crafting my legacy through calloused hands and unwavering focus. My drive to outwork everyone else wasn't about competition; it was about proving that my differences had forged something unstoppable.

I threw myself into work, climbing the ranks by **age 23**, as if success could patch the holes in my foundation. For a while, I thought I had outrun my past. Life has a way of stress-testing our repairs, however, and when my wife handed me divorce papers that Christmas of '98, everything I'd built began to crack.

The darkness I thought I'd left behind in childhood came roaring back. There I was, **27** years old and successful on paper, but sitting on my bed with a gun in my mouth. It took my ex-wife's screams and the thought of my four-year-old daughter to pull me back from that edge. For three years after this moment, my little girl's face was the only light I could see.

That's the thing about childhood trauma - it doesn't just vanish when you get taller. It shapes how you love, how you parent, and how you survive. My wife had her own demons, I later learned. We were two broken people without the right tools, trying to build something whole. Growing up doesn't fix what's broken. It just gives you new rooms in which to store your pain. But sometimes, in those rooms, you find reasons to heal. My daughter became mine.

At **28** my battles continued while I faced bankruptcy and a traumatic divorce, but amidst the darkness, I found a way to break free. In the end, survival transformed into triumph, not because I finally fit in, but because I finally understood this truth:

Sometimes the path to belonging isn't about changing who you are; it's about finding where your differences become your strengths, the champion spirit within. And now I want to share this method with you.

This **four-step** process has become my lifeline, teaching me how to confront the shadows of my past, master my emotions, and view my life through a new lens. I set goals and achieved them, gaining a power I never knew I had.

If you've faced childhood abuse, emotional neglect, or the suffocating weight of shame, anger, depression, and low self-worth, this book is for you. If you long to feel the freedom of true happiness for the first time, to embrace your authentic self, know that you are not alone. I understand the turmoil within; I've walked that painful path and emerged stronger. Every day, I apply these steps to my life, and am now living my best life. Together, we can heal and rediscover the joy we deserve.

Remember: Expect more from yourself than you do from others. You have everything to win inside of you. Yes, you! The Champion Spirit!

Index

Chapter 1: Facing Your Trauma

I will guide you through the act that helps you acknowledge and process the trauma you've been carrying, the first step to healing.

Chapter 2: Mirror Time/ Visualization

These moments are your chance to plant seeds that will bloom into a life of healing and peace, and there's one practice, one minute of "mirror time," that can be one of your most powerful tools.

Chapter 3: Gratitude & Journaling

Giving thanks increases happiness, improves sleep, supports heart health, reduces stress levels, and improves life satisfaction. By incorporating a gratitude journal into your daily life, you can experience these benefits and improve your overall well-being.

Chapter 4: Autohypnosis

I will guide you through a step-by-step process to explain why and how auto hypnosis is crucial for overcoming complex childhood trauma. You will learn how to reprogram your subconscious mind while you sleep, setting the foundation for profound healing.

Chapter 5: Triggers /A Bad Day

Here, I'll guide you through a step-by-step process that explains the why and how of harnessing the power of self-hypnosis. You will learn when to turn to it and how it can steady you after life's inevitable potholes shatter your tranquility.

Chapter 1
Facing your Trauma

Truth: This is where change begins. When you revisit trauma, memories and feelings will flood back with such intensity that you might feel transported back to that moment. Be gentle with yourself during this process. **Your mind and body remember, and that's normal. You are not alone in this fight!**

Today marks a turning point. Feel these words deep in your bones: This is both an ending and a beginning. Here ends the cycle of self-destruction the harsh inner voice, the constant doubt, the feeling that you don't belong. No more drowning in unworthiness. No more believing you're not enough. From this moment forward, you rise. You are worthy. You are here. You belong. Let that truth burn brightly and fiercely within you.

Choose Option A or Option B: Both exercises work best in a private setting.

Option A: Write a Letter

Find a quiet, secluded place where you feel safe to explore your feelings. Write a letter to yourself. Freely express your thoughts. Don't worry about how it sounds; this is your space.

Consider the following steps as you write:

1. **Address your abuser**(s) by name. Tell them what they did and how it made you feel. Be specific about the details.

2. **Describe the traumatic event or events**. Start by describing the traumatic events in the order they occurred as best you can. Try to remember as many details as possible. What happened? Who was there? Where were you? The more specific you can be, the better.

3. **Tell them how it hurt you and robbed you of joy!** Be specific about the pain they caused. How did their actions make you feel about yourself? What beliefs did you form as a result? Let them know the full weight of the hurt they inflicted. Let them know what you feel you've missed out on because of what they did. This letter is your chance to release the feelings you've been carrying, the anger, the sadness, the fear. Let it all out. Don't hold anything back. This is for your healing, your release. This is where the healing starts. I believe in you. You can be explicit. Speak your truth and express your emotions freely.

4. **Destroy the Letter**. Once you've written everything down, it's time to let it go. Destroy the letter in whatever way feels most symbolic to you. This is your act of release, of finally letting go of the trauma that's held you back for so long.

Reminder: You should never approach, speak to, or even think your abuser will apologize. Don't waste your energy hoping for an apology that will never come. Some people never acknowledge the harm they've caused, and by holding onto that expectation you stay chained to the past. Your peace and healing doesn't depend on them. Focus on moving forward. You are more than what they did to you, and your healing doesn't need their permission.

After writing, you may experience intense emotions or feel drained. Whatever you feel is valid. Revisiting these memories can be challenging for your mind and body, and it's normal to feel physical fatigue.

This is the first step toward healing complex trauma. After completing the exercise, take care of yourself. Consider napping, going for a walk, calling a loved one, or drawing a soothing bath-whatever feels like an act of kindness toward yourself. You deserve great things in this life!

Continue to practice self-care in the days that follow. Remember, you don't have to carry the emotions from your writing into the rest of your day. You can return to this exercise whenever you need to.

Remember this moment. Change unfolds with a single brave step forward your step, your choice, your new beginning. The path ahead starts right here, right now, with you.

Option B: Demonstrative Activity

Find a quiet, secluded place where you feel safe to explore your feelings. Freely express your thoughts. Don't worry about how it sounds; this is your space.

Place a pillow or stuffed animal in a chair. Sit or stand across from it, whichever feels most comfortable. As you engage in this exercise, refer to the pillow or stuffed animal by the name of your abuser(s).

Be open to expressing all your emotions and feelings toward this object. While it may feel silly, the act of releasing your emotions onto the object allows you to break free from the years of emotional blocks you have built.

At the Pillow or Stuffed Animal (or another inanimate object)

1. **Address your abuser**(s) by name. Tell them what they did and how it made you feel. Be specific about the details.

2. **Describe the traumatic event** or events. Start by describing the traumatic events in the order they occurred, as best you can. Try to remember as many details as possible. What happened? Who was there? Where were you? The more specific you can be, the better.

3. **Tell them how it hurt you and robbed you of joy!** Be specific about the pain they caused. How did their actions make you feel about yourself? What beliefs did you form as a result? Let them know the full weight of the hurt they inflicted. Let them know what you feel you've missed out on because of what they did. This activity is your chance to release the feelings you've been carrying, the anger, the sadness, the fear. Let it all out. Don't hold anything back. This is for your healing, your release.

Reminder: You should never approach, speak to, or even think your abuser will apologize. Don't waste your energy hoping for an apology that will never come. Some people never acknowledge the harm they've caused, and by holding onto that expectation you stay chained to the past. Your peace and healing doesn't depend on them. Focus on moving forward. You are more than what they did to you, and your healing doesn't need their permission.

After this demonstration you may experience intense emotions or feel drained. Whatever you feel is valid. Revisiting these memories can be challenging for your mind and body, and it's normal to feel physical fatigue.

This is the first step toward healing complex trauma. After completing the exercise, take care of yourself. Consider napping, going for a walk, calling a loved one, or drawing a soothing bath- whatever feels like an act of kindness toward yourself. You deserve great things in this life!

Continue to practice self-care in the days that follow. Remember, you don't have to carry the emotions from your writing into the rest of your day. You can return to this exercise whenever you need to.

Remember this moment. Change unfolds with a single brave step forward - your step, your choice, your new beginning. The path ahead starts right here, right now, with you.

Healing Factor: Both exercises offer a path to gently acknowledge and process the trauma you've been carrying. Each one provides a safe way to explore and understand experiences that have shaped you, moving at your own pace.

You deserve amazing things in life. I believe in you, and now it's time for you to start believing in yourself. I encourage you to take your time. Move at your own pace. Let your emotions and feelings flow. As you do, you will start to feel a weightlifting; you'll start to feel yourself coming alive. This is the first step in healing from past trauma and stepping into the life you've always deserved.

I've walked this path. I've felt the healing. There was a time when the pain of my past felt like a weight I couldn't escape, when I didn't know how to break free. I want you to know the power of this process, of putting your trauma into words and then letting it go. I want you to experience the recovery that comes from acknowledging your pain and releasing it. It's through this act of bravery and vulnerability that you'll find peace. I believe in you.

If you require additional support with this step, please refer to the website for further resources and examples.

Oakironbrotherhood.com Oakironbrotherhood@gmail.com

Chapter 2
Mirror Time

When you wake up and get out of bed, your subconscious mind is open and especially impressionable. These first ten minutes are a vital time to reprogram your thoughts through intentional repetition of affirmations. This will take only a minute of your time each morning.

1. Stand a few inches from the mirror.
2. Lift your head and take a few slow, deep breaths.
3. Focus your gaze. If it feels easier, concentrate on just one eye.
4. Look deeply into your eye(s) and speak, whether aloud or silently. Say what you need to hear and speak with feeling. It's okay to smile at yourself, too! Allow your words to flow over you like a warm shower, gently soaking in.

ME: I wrote 10 affirmations on an index card and repeated them to myself in the mirror three times each morning. Commit to doing it for one month and see how you feel. You might be surprised at the shift in your mindset. Remember. I believe in you! You can do this. **You are VALUABLE; you are WORTHY, AND you DESERVE great things in this life!!**

Here are some examples:

- Good morning, I love you. I am valuable. I deserve great things in this life.
- I am smart. I am wise. I am intelligent.
- I am happy. I am strong, I am healthy.
- I am worthy.
- I am positive. I am energetic.

The Power of Consistent Repetition

The key to this practice is repetition with intention. This is a powerful moment where you reinforce the positive messages you're working to internalize, complementing the autohypnosis you practiced the night before. (We will discuss this in the final chapter.)

Reminder: The lies of our past have been ingrained in us through years of repetition, so it's only through **consistent, intentional repetition** of truth that we'll rewire our minds and heal. Repetition is the mother of learning, and when it comes to healing from trauma, this couldn't be truer.

Healing Factor: By using visualization and positive affirmations, you can experience the transformation that comes through reprogramming from speaking truth into your own soul.

*Remember this moment:

You. Yes, you. THIS is your moment of power. Standing before the mirror, eyes locked with your reflection, you see that **champion** spirit burning within. This isn't just another morning; this is where you are laying the blueprint for today.

Mirror Time

This quiet moment might be the only time today you'll hear words that lift your soul. The hours ahead? They might not shower you with joy, but remember, it's more than okay to celebrate yourself. It's more than okay to recognize your worth. It's more than okay to know just how valuable you truly are.

And yes, **you** deserve to have a great day. You deserve great things in this life. Not because you've earned it, but because greatness lives in your DNA. This is your time to shine-not tomorrow, not someday, but right now. Claim it. Own it. Live it.

I encourage you not to miss this moment. Do not miss the chance to reinforce the positive messages you're working to internalize! I believe in you!

Oakironbrotherhood.com Oakironbrotherhood@gmail.com

Chapter 3
Gratitude

Daily journaling opens a gateway to gratitude, but speaking your thanks—whether aloud or silently—amplifies its power. Each morning, I kneel in humble appreciation, my heart overflowing with thankfulness for my wife, children, friends, job, and health.

I clasp my hands together, touching my thumbs to my lips in prayer. In my mind's eye, I'm kneeling before Jesus's throne, kissing His hand in deepest gratitude. This daily ritual has become my anchor, my reminder of life's countless blessings.

Think about it: You open your eyes in the morning. Your lungs draw breath. Your legs carry you forward. Your eyes take in the world's beauty. Your mind dreams, thinks, and creates. Even now, as you read these words, you're experiencing the gift of consciousness.

We all have something to be thankful for every single day. Sometimes it's the grand moments that take our breath away. Other times, it's the simple miracle of being alive. The key is recognizing these blessings, no matter their size.

Healing Factor: I pray you will make giving thanks a daily exercise. Giving thanks increases happiness, improves sleep, supports heart health, and reduces stress levels, and improves life satisfaction. Gratitude will help you with everyday life.

This journal takes a few minutes a day to write down the things for which you are thankful. By incorporating gratitude into your daily life, you can experience these benefits and improve your overall well-being. This helps you focus on the positive and reflect on your blessings.

I started simply. Each morning, I wrote "I'm so happy and grateful." That single line became my foundation. As days passed, this small practice grew into a natural daily habit. Soon, I found myself excited to put my gratitude on paper.

1. Challenge yourself for the first seven days to write for two minutes. You have this time, so make time.
2. Start Small (like, really small) Make it so easy you can't talk yourself out of it.
3. Make It Real, Not Perfect. This is your mind and your life. It's you and only you.
4. Mix Up Your Methods. Don't feel stuck with just journaling. You might:

   - Take a quick photo of something you're grateful for.
   - Send a thank-you text to yourself. That's right to you.
   - Just pause for 10 seconds to give thanks inside or out loud.
   - Speak your thanks aloud or silently (amplifying its power) while you're in the shower or standing in front of your mirror or driving to work.

5. The Two-Minute Rule: Keep it brief. If it takes longer than two minutes, you're probably making it too complicated. Quick hits of gratitude are often more sustainable than lengthy sessions.

Gratitude

Make it **personal to you**. If you hate writing, don't force yourself to keep a journal. If you're not a morning person, do it at lunch. The best gratitude practice is one you'll actually stick with.

Remember: Speak with feeling! Psalms 15 says, "Keep your word to yourself." The cool thing about gratitude is that it's like a muscle – the more you use it, the stronger it gets.

On the following pages, you'll find a sample journal. Yours does not have to look like mine or anyone else's. Make it your own. You can use a special journal, a simple notebook, or even a digital app. However, if it's easier, start here by copying these phrases.

I am smart,

_____

I am valuable,

_____

I am worthy of

_____

I am truly grateful for

I am so happy and grateful

I am happy

I am healty

I am intelligent

I am wise

I am peaceful

I am thankful for

Chapter 4
Autohypnosis: The How and Why

I will guide you through a step-by-step process to explain why and how auto hypnosis is crucial for overcoming complex childhood trauma. You will learn how to reprogram your subconscious mind while you sleep, setting the foundation for profound healing.

Your trauma will relapse unless you replace it.

Autohypnosis is a powerful tool for transforming your subconscious mind. Through **repetition**, you will remap and reprogram your subconscious, replacing negative thought patterns with positive ones and rewriting harmful programming that's holding you back. Think of your mind as a supercomputer and autohypnosis as the software update it needs to run optimally.

Neuroscientists have discovered that the adult subconscious mind is most receptive to reprogramming twice a day. Let's explore these two optimal times and what occurs throughout them.

During both waking and sleeping states, your brain produces various types of electrical waves. Among these are theta waves and alpha waves. Theta, the slower of the two, is particularly significant. These slower brain waves emerge when you are lightly sleeping, dreaming, or in deep relaxation. Experts believe theta waves play a crucial role in processing information and **forming memories.**

Simply put, it is during the first five minutes of sleep that your subconscious mind opens the door for remapping and reprogramming.

1. As you wake up and get out of bed, your subconscious remains open for reprogramming. The first ten minutes are crucial for reshaping your automatic thought patterns through repetition.
2. Autohypnosis allows you to install a new program in your life, like upgrading a computer's hard drive with new software.

Reminder: You have the power to rewrite any program in your life.

Healing Factor: Remapping and reprogramming your subconscious mind through autohypnosis will help replace trauma. If trauma resurfaces in your life, it may indicate that you have not fully replaced it. The key to healing is to replace your trauma with positive affirmations, achieved through consistent repetition. Input what you want to replace the trauma, and repeat it during those crucial waking moments and just before you go to sleep.

Growing up, I was often labeled as dumb and stupid. Through the process of remapping my subconscious, trauma-driven thinking, I transformed my life with positive affirmations and now know the truth. I am not dumb and stupid. I am smart and intelligent.

This step is vital for overcoming your childhood complex trauma. The following guide to self-hypnosis offers a method for reprogramming your subconscious mind while you sleep. Each night, I go to sleep with my headphones on, listening to recordings of myself. When I wake up, I'm still listening to my own voice. This is my daily routine for a reason. **Repetition** is the key to instigating change in the subconscious mind.

Auto-Hypnosis Guidelines

Headphones: While not required, headphones are recommended for a more immersive experience.

Autohypnosis: The How and Why

Recording Your Affirmations

A. Use a voice recorder on your phone or listening device to create a recording of yourself for yourself. I recommend recording your own voice. Think about this: your brain is familiar with your voice. You will find it challenging in the beginning. That's normal.

1. When recording, speak slowly and let your words flow naturally, as if you're having a conversation. Think of it as a list of what you feel is missing in your life and within yourself. My personal recording lasts between 2 to 6 minutes and features soft background music.

2. As you prepare for bed, clear your mind. Practice mindfulness or meditation to set the stage for listening to your recording as you fall asleep. Start simply. The most basic way to practice mindfulness is through breathing. Begin with 10 to 20 conscious breaths, letting each inhale and exhale calm your body. As you breathe, gently release negative thoughts and open yourself to positivity. Choose one clear image to anchor your mind such as a vibrant red rose. See yourself holding it. Let your attention trace the delicate texture of each petal, feeling their silken ripples beneath your fingertips. Breathe in its sweet fragrance. Notice how the sturdy green stem supports this delicate bloom. In this quiet space, focusing on a single beautiful object, your mind naturally settles into stillness. This is mindfulness at its purest - one breath, one image, one moment of complete presence.

When recording, speak slowly and let your words flow naturally, as if you're having a conversation. Think of it as a list of what you feel is missing in your life and within yourself. My personal recording lasts between 2 to 6 minutes and features soft background music.

Examples:

- "I am smart. I am intelligent. I am wise. I am creative. I believe in myself. I deserve great things in this life." *pause, count silently. 1.2.3.*
- "I am loved. I am calm. I am confident. I am peaceful... " *pause, count 1.2.3.*
- "I am happy. I am funny. I am strong. I am handsome... " *pause ... 1. 2. 3.*
- "I am grateful. I am positive. I am thankful. I am energetic... "*pause]. 2. 3.*
- "I am whole. I am perfect. I am harmonious. I am kind... " *pause. 1.2.3.*

Dreaming: If you wake up from dreaming, pay attention! Dreaming signifies that you are building a new mental road, and it's time to continue constructing this path. You may need to adjust your recording by adding or deleting certain words or phrases. Your mind has unlimited avenues to explore. Your mind is a supercomputer. By embracing this process, you can begin to reshape your life and heal from past traumas.

Remember this crucial truth: If you don't actively remap or replace your trauma, it will return with a **vengeance**. This isn't just about healing; it's about complete transformation.

Chapter 5
When the Triggers Come/ When You've Had a Bad Day

L ife is unpredictable and will throw challenges your way. However, there is a powerful tool to help you navigate these obstacles and keep you on your path of healing. Self-hypnosis.

This process is your anchor, your key to maintaining hard-won progress. With self-hypnosis in your toolkit, you'll have the strength to keep moving forward, no matter what comes your way. And that's how you'll continue your journey, the journey to reclaim the peace and happiness that's rightfully yours.

Triggers can arise unexpectedly, often in response to a conversation or situation, and they stem from unresolved childhood trauma. These triggers reflect subconscious patterns and self-images shaped by your past experiences.

1. Understanding the Triggers

When you experience a trigger, it signifies that you are beginning to remap and reprogram your subconscious mind.

2. Why This Happens

You might have been making progress with positive thinking, only to encounter a setback, a pothole in your path. Your brain instinctively fights this change, preferring the familiarity of negative thinking. This resistance is rooted in the trauma that remains unaddressed and **unprogrammed**.

3. Cleaning Out the Closet

Think of this process as cleaning out a closet. You're working to replace old, negative patterns with new, positive repetitions. To move forward, you must engage in this practice **daily**.

Imagine standing waist-deep in the ocean, attempting to walk toward the shore. Just as a wave can push you back, **your mind** will initially resist this change. It's essential to persist, repeating your affirmations day after day to effectively remap your subconscious.

You will encounter setbacks on your journey to becoming the person you are meant to be. Your brain may cling to its old ways but remember **failure does not equate to defeat**. You might grapple with self-doubt, feeling frustrated or ashamed, convinced that you have failed. These feelings are echoes of the negative beliefs you accepted as a child, now ingrained in your subconscious. **Today is a New Day**

Getting back on Track 1: Take Small Steps

Begin with small, manageable actions. Celebrate your progress, no matter how minor. For **example**, after making a cup of coffee, acknowledge your achievement: "I did a good job making that coffee," or "I am great at making my bed." These simple acknowledgments will gradually shift your thinking.

As your day unfolds, recognize, and affirm your accomplishments. Remind yourself of the simplest achievements. This practice will help you build a positive mindset, and before you know it, you'll find yourself back on track.

Getting Back on Track 2

Feed your subconscious mind with new and positive thoughts. Just like a car will run poorly if you put in bad gas, your mind needs quality input to function well.

You will also benefit from creating or listening to affirmation recordings or repeating them aloud.

UNDER NO CIRCUMSTANCES DENY WHAT YOU HAVE AFFIRMED!

Example: A

Today is my day-the start of my new life. I feel the vibrant energy of success flowing through me right now. I am limitless, and I believe fully in myself. I am loveable, I am beautiful, and I radiate positive energy. Today, I embrace my incredible potential. I am smart, I am intelligent, and I am wise. Confidence fills me. I am powerful, I am strong, and I am happy.

I carry peace and calm within me, and there are no limits to what I can achieve. I excel at my work, and negativity has no power over me. I rise above it, seeing it only as a test of my strength. Doubt has no place here-I am in control of my thoughts and emotions. Today is a great day, and I am unstoppable.

Example: B

Your recording might be this short. Mine was!

I believe in myself. I am positive. I am strong. I am happy. Negativity is just a test. I am positive. I am strong. I am happy. I believe in myself.

In my first 30 days of applying these steps. I probably listened to myself 100 different times.

These three steps have changed my life. They can change your life. I believe in you; you can do this.

Embrace the journey ahead and remember that your affirmations are powerful. You can rewrite your story, one positive thought at a time.

Reminder: **Failure does not equate defeat**. It takes time to reprogram your subconscious mind. It must be through **repetition**.

Remember this crucial truth:

If you're reading this part, it means you've hit a pothole. And you know what? That's perfectly okay. You're still moving forward. A bump in the road doesn't define your journey.

Sometimes it's going to feel like you can't get anything right. Trust me, I've been there! But here's the truth: That resistance you're feeling? It's actually a sign of progress. Your mind is fighting you every step of the way because it's desperately clinging to what's familiar, your old patterns and comfortable habits. Celebrate this struggle. Yes, celebrate it! This discomfort means you're changing, evolving, becoming someone new. This isn't failure; this is transformation in action. And transformation? It's never comfortable, but it's always worth it.

You have found the Champion Spirit within!

Oakironbrotherhood.com Oakironbrotherhood@gmail.com

To God, My Wife, and Those Who Saved Me

There was a time when darkness wasn't just around me, it was inside me. Hope felt like a foreign language I couldn't speak, and love seemed like a distant star I could never reach. But **God**, in His infinite wisdom, never abandoned me, even when I couldn't feel His presence. He was painting a masterpiece while I was staring at a blank canvas.

To my wife: You taught me that grace isn't just a word in prayer, it's in the way you looked at me when I couldn't look at myself. Your love became the lighthouse that guided me home when I was lost at sea. You saw beauty in my broken pieces and showed me that scars can be stories of survival, not just reminders of pain.

To my friends from school: You'll never know how those simple moments in hallways and classrooms breathed life back into my soul. Each laugh we shared, each conversation that made me feel seen—they were building blocks, slowly reconstructing my sense of worth. In those hours between bells, you made me feel like I belonged somewhere in this vast world.

And to my three **best friends**—my anchors, my brothers: You didn't just share your lives with me; you showed me that life was worth living. When I was hanging by a thread, you became the hands that held me up. Your friendship wasn't just a gift, it was oxygen when I was drowning.

I stand here today because of a divine tapestry woven with God's grace, my wife's love, and your unwavering friendship. You didn't just change my life, you saved it. With eternal gratitude, Thank you, God! PS. AG. SE.LS.

Bonnie H, The Editor: Thank you for your time, your patience, and your belief in this big country guy. I never imagined I'd write a book, let alone publish one. And yet, here we are—crafting a legacy that aims to help others find freedom from their trauma. Your support is helping pave the way for people to discover what a joyful life can truly look like.

Troy: Thank you for understanding me in a way only another man can. For that, I'm grateful.

Frank & Wife, your prayers and encouragement helped me see the bigger picture when I needed it most.

Tommy and Pam, your consistent prayers and shared wisdom have meant more than words can express. With deepest appreciation, thank you for believing in me.

This book— the journey you are about to embark on—has been walked by many men in silence before you, and many will follow, concealing their pain. I present these steps to you now, not as definitive answers but as invitations. Not as a map, but as a light to guide you when the path grows dark.

May **God** watch over you and protect you, Amen.

This book is **my promise:** each step battle-tested, each practice proven in the trenches of trauma. They worked for someone who was told they shouldn't even be alive. They'll work for you too—no matter how shattered you feel, no matter how many pieces you think you're in.

Oakironbrotherhood.com Oakironbrotherhood@gmail.com

The champion spirit lives within you.

www.ingramcontent.com/pod-product-compliance
Lightning Source LLC
Chambersburg PA
CBHW051650120626
46551CB00015B/2302